JAPAN

© Aladdin Books Ltd 1988

Designed and produced by
Aladdin Books Ltd
70 Old Compton Street
London W1

First published in
Great Britain in 1988 by
Franklin Watts
12a Golden Square
London W1

ISBN 0 86313 700 8

Printed in Belgium

Design   David West
                  Children's Book Design

Editor   Denny Robson

Researcher   Cecilia Weston-Baker

Illustrator   Rob Shone

Consultant   Richard Tames,
                  School of Oriental
                  and African Studies,
                  University of London.

CONTENTS

GREAT CIVILIZATIONS

JAPAN

5000 BC–TODAY

Mavis Pilbeam

FRANKLIN WATTS

London · New York · Toronto · Sydney

INTRODUCTION

A Japanese myth tells how Amaterasu, the Sun Goddess, was angry with her brother the Storm God. She hid in a cave. Darkness fell. The other gods gathered outside the cave and hung a jewel and a mirror in the sacred tree. A goddess did a funny dance to make them all laugh. Amaterasu heard, peeped out and saw her bright face in the mirror. She came out further to have a closer look. A god quickly closed up the mouth of the cave and the sun shone again.

Japan is a small but rich island country in the Far East of Asia. It is a varied, living civilization which has ancient roots. Its written history dates back to Chinese historians writing in the first century AD. Almost throughout its history Japan has been independent of other countries. But the people have always been curious about the outside world. For almost 2,000 years they have borrowed ideas from China and Korea, Europe and the United States. However, they always change things to suit their tastes, so their way of life and arts have a strong Japanese flavour. The people have a keen sense of order and a love of nature, beauty and perfection, shown in the way they live and work.

Ancient myths tell of the founding of Japan and its imperial family. Over the centuries there have been many power struggles but the original imperial family still survives. It is a link with the past in this modern industrialised country.

This book divides Japan's history into four parts. First Japan changes slowly from a country of scattered tribes to a nation ruled by an emperor. Next comes a period of civil wars during which the Europeans arrive. Then Japan shuts out the outside world and peacefully develops its own arts and society. Lastly Japan changes to a country committed to a policy of modernization and becomes a strong and prosperous world power.

THE MAKING OF JAPAN

Japanese civilization began to develop very slowly from about 5,000 BC when people started to make pottery. Around 300 BC new ideas came from the Asian mainland about rice-growing and how to make metal tools and swords. Chinese writers of the time described how the many small clans in Japan were fighting for power. Eventually, one strong Japanese leader took control in about AD 400. The emperors are his descendants. The capital was set up in Yamato province in the west. Then more settlers began to move slowly to the east.

Life became peaceful. Japan learned many things from China about government, Buddhist religion and the arts. The emperors built fine capital cities, temples and palaces. Gradually, however, the emperors became weak and real power fell into the hands of warrior leaders.

5000 BC-AD1192

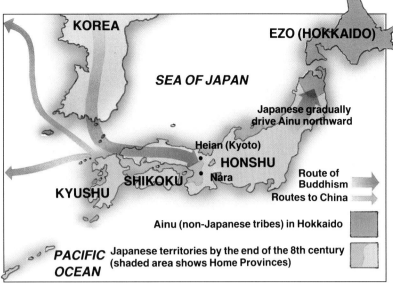

KOREA

EZO (HOKKAIDO)

SEA OF JAPAN

Japanese gradually drive Ainu northward

Heian (Kyoto)

HONSHU

Nara

SHIKOKU

KYUSHU

Route of Buddhism

Routes to China

Ainu (non-Japanese tribes) in Hokkaido

PACIFIC OCEAN

Japanese territories by the end of the 8th century (shaded area shows Home Provinces)

In the Heian period, from AD 794 to 1192, the imperial court was one of the most elegant in Japanese history. An aristocratic family named Fujiwara advised the emperor and arranged his entertainments. At New Year there was the annual archery contest.

DATECHART

c10,000 BC-300 BC People live by hunting and fishing. Primitive pottery becomes more sophisticated and people begin to live in huts.

c300 BC-AD 300 A different style of pottery appears. There are bronze and iron objects and rice-growing.

AD 57 Japanese messengers visit China, beginning 800 years of Chinese influence.

cAD 300-552 The Japanese imperial family becomes established in Yamato. Emperors and empresses are buried in tombs covered by huge mounds.

cAD 450 Introduction of Chinese writing.

AD 594 Buddhism becomes the state religion supported by Shotoku Taishi.

AD 645 A new Chinese-style central government is set up.

AD 710 New capital at Nara.

AD 752 The Todaiji Buddha is made.

AD 794 New capital at Heian.

cAD 894 End of first period of Chinese influence.

AD 858 The Fujiwara family starts to gain power.

cAD 1010 Murasaki Shikibu writes *The Tale of Genji*.

AD 1160 The kidnapping of Goshirakawa.

AD 1180-1185 The Gempei War: the Taira family are defeated by Minamoto Yoritomo and his clan. He starts an age of military rule.

The early settlements

The early Japanese lived by hunting and fishing. Rice-growing started about 300 BC. It was very hard work. The rice had to be planted in flooded fields with banks around them to keep the water in. At harvest time whole villages would work together in a group.

For a long time taxes were paid in rice instead of money. One *koku* of rice was the amount eaten by one man in a year. A man's wealth was measured by the number of *koku* he could grow on his land.

Japanese people still eat rice every day. They also like to work in groups, just as their ancestors did when cutting rice. In modern times machines have made rice-growing much easier.

Early potters made cooking pots, storage jars, funeral urns and clay objects for religious rites. The pots were probably coil pots like those in the picture. At first pots were decorated with curved lines and rope patterns. Simpler forms came in after 300 BC.

Shinto religion

The oldest religion in Japan is called Shinto, which means "The Way of the Gods". The Japanese used to believe that every natural thing – tree, river or mountain – was the home of a god. They built holy places for them called shrines. Today Japanese people still visit shrines, especially at New Year, to pray for good fortune and health. Most people have a Shinto wedding and enjoy festivals for the gods.

   The first emperor, Jimmu, was said to be descended from the Sun Goddess, who gave him Three Sacred Treasures: a Mirror, a Sword and a Jewel. They are kept in the Ise Shrine, shown in the picture. This shrine is rebuilt every 20 years. The priestesses' costumes have not changed for 1200 years.

Burials

The power and wealth of the early emperors was shown by the enormous burial mounds called *Kofun* which covered their tombs. The tomb of Emperor Nintoku in the photograph is 486 metres long and is shaped like a giant keyhole. Around the mounds were rows of *haniwa*. *Haniwa* were clay models of warriors, horsemen, courtiers and court ladies. They acted as guards and servants for the dead man. Stately dances were performed at the funerals.

9

Chinese influences

In AD 57 Japanese messengers were sent to China. For the next 800 years the Japanese borrowed many Chinese ideas. A Chinese-style government and tax system were set up. Capital cities were planned like the Chinese city Changan. Chinese learning and arts also came to Japan.

The religion of Buddhism started in India and came to Japan through China and Korea in the 6th century. A powerful statesman called Shotoku Taishi welcomed Buddhist monks to the court. Many temples were built and most people belonged to both Shinto and Buddhism. Todaiji temple in Nara contains a bronze statue of Buddha 16 metres high (right).

Writing

The Japanese started using the Chinese writing system in the 5th century. They added two sets of new letters so that they could write down the Japanese language. The writing was done with a brush and ink on fine paper. It became very important for people to have good handwriting.

Around AD 1010 a court lady called Murasaki Shikibu wrote a famous story called *The Tale of Genji*. It tells of the life and loves of a handsome, clever Heian nobleman called Genji, "The Shining Prince".

源氏

Gen – ji

Warrior monk   Buddhist Prince   Nobleman   Nobleman's wife   Children of noble family

The nobility

The nobility of the Heian period were descendants of clan chieftains of earlier times. They worked as officials in the emperor's court. The Fujiwara became the most powerful by marrying their daughters to different emperors.

Heian, later called Kyoto, was in one of the five Home Provinces. The nobles all wanted to live in or near Heian. They thought that people who lived outside this area were barbarians who only existed to grow rice and pay taxes.

Court life was very formal. Children rarely saw their parents. But the nobility loved beautiful things, elegant clothes and nature. In this narrow world a very special Japanese culture grew up.

The end of the Heian period

In the 12th century some emperors gave up ruling and became priests, or "cloistered emperors". They tried to control the new young emperor from behind the scenes.

Two big warrior families, the Minamoto and the Taira, began to compete for power. At the same time the emperors began to quarrel with the Fujiwara courtiers who advised them.

A cloistered emperor called Goshirakawa was captured by the Minamoto and Fujiwara. There was war between the Minamoto and the Taira and the Minamoto won.

THE AGE OF STRIFE 1192-1603

In 1192 Minamoto Yoritomo became military ruler, or Shogun. He set up his military government, the Shogunate, in Kamakura. For the next seven centuries the shoguns were the real rulers of Japan. The emperors remained in Kyoto, powerless. But later shoguns were not so strong. Local lords called *daimyo* set themselves up in authority in each district. Every *daimyo* had a private army of *samurai* warriors. This led to the Age of Strife with everyone fighting for survival, and central government lost control.

Even so, arts and religion flourished. Zen Buddhism, which taught a simple way of life, was introduced from China. Trade and industry also increased. Eventually three great leaders came forward one after the other: Oda Nobunaga, Toyotomi Hideyoshi and Tokugawa Ieyasu. They succeeded in unifying Japan.

Fierce invaders from China called Mongols attacked Japan in 1274. The *samurai* warriors fought them off and built great walls for defence. The Mongols came again but a great storm wrecked their ships.

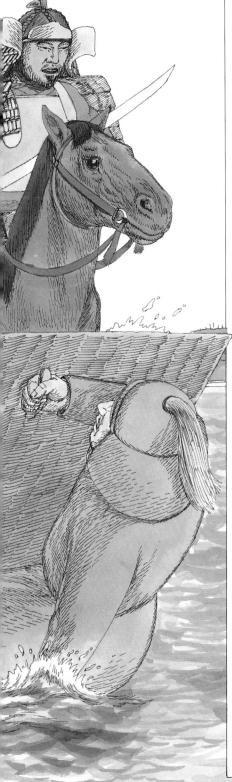

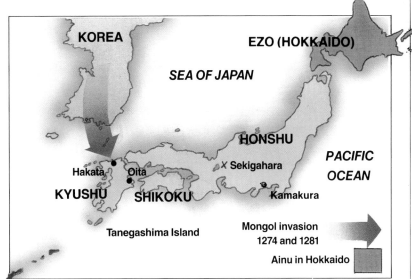

KOREA

EZO (HOKKAIDO)

SEA OF JAPAN

HONSHU

PACIFIC OCEAN

X Sekigahara

Hakata Oita

KYUSHU SHIKOKU

Kamakura

Tanegashima Island

Mongol invasion 1274 and 1281

Ainu in Hokkaido

DATECHART

1192 The Kamakura Shogunate is established by Minamoto Yoritomo. He appoints provincial officials.

1190s The monk Eisai brings Zen Buddhism from China. The Zen arts of tea ceremony, flower arrangement and ink-painting grow in Japan.

1274 and 1281 Mongol invasions.

1338 Ashikaga family establishes Shogunate headquarters in Kyoto.

1401 New government contacts and trade with China.

1467 A series of wars leads to the Age of Strife.

1543 Arrival of first Portuguese at Tanegashima. Introduction of guns.

1549 St Francis Xavier preaches Christianity.

1568-1576 The first great leader and general, Oda Nobunaga, overthrows the Shogunate and wins the Battle of Nagashino. For thirty years there is no Shogun as the fight for leadership continues.

1570s The Portuguese move to Nagasaki port.

1576 Nobunaga builds Azuchi castle.

1582 Nobunaga is murdered by a traitor.

1590 The second leader, the general Toyotomi Hideyoshi, unifies Japan.

1592 and 1597 Invasions of Korea end in failure.

1600 William Adams, first Englishman in Japan, is shipwrecked at Oita.

1600 The third leader, Tokugawa Ieyasu, establishes his power at the Battle of Sekigahara.

The shoguns
Early shoguns guarded Japan's frontiers from the Ainu, non-Japanese people living in the north. But with the arrival of Minamoto Yoritomo, shoguns became military dictators. This meant they controlled the emperors and ruled the whole country through their officials.

Minamoto Yoritomo had fought in his first battle at the age of thirteen. His headquarters were at Kamakura. In the picture, the Shogun is receiving some visitors very formally. His sword-bearer sits to his left. Guards hide behind sliding doors to leap out at the first sign of trouble.

The common people
The lives of the farmers and other workers were ruled by the *daimyo*. Forestry, mining for gold and local industries such as paper-making became important at this time.

Life was hard. Sometimes farmers rebelled and tried to run away, especially if there was a poor harvest. However, farming people enjoyed dancing and drinking *sake* (rice wine) at festival time.

Taxes were paid in *koku* of rice. The *koku* were taken on horseback to the *daimyo*'s steward. The steward made calculations of what was owed on his abacus and a scribe wrote down the accounts.

Swordmakers
Swordmakers were the top craftsmen. They used their secret skills to beat the finest steel into the sharpest blades. A *samurai* always carried two swords. They were his most precious possessions.

Samurai
The *samurai* were warriors who served the shogun or *daimyo*. They swore loyalty to their masters and would gladly die for them. It is said they never complained about hardships and never broke a promise.

Martial arts such as *judo* and *kendo* (fencing) began as *samurai* fighting skills. Although they were fierce warriors the *samurai* led simple lives. They followed a new kind of Buddhism called Zen. They often sat cross-legged in meditation.

Fishing
Fishing became important at this time and fish has been a popular food in Japan ever since. In the photograph below, modern fishermen sort through the night's catch.

A *samurai* warrior in full armour

THE AGE OF STRIFE

Castles

As the *daimyo* grew more powerful, many of them built castles to show their strength. The castles were built on mounds faced with stone and they had wooden towers. There were narrow slits for windows through which defenders shot arrows or bullets when they were under attack.

Castle towns grew up round the castles. Many of these towns, such as Osaka, are now important centres. The photograph shows Osaka castle. Many of the castles today are modern concrete copies of originals.

Some towns had weekly markets, or, if they were on the coast, they developed into ports. Ships sailed between the ports or went overseas for trade. As the towns became important cities, the influence of the central government was forgotten.

Christianity and guns

In the 16th century Portuguese, Spanish, Dutch and English traders sailed far and wide to find wealth. The Portuguese were the first to arrive in Japan. The Japanese were fascinated by these tall men with long noses and baggy trousers, who spoke an unknown language and came from an unknown land.

The Portuguese are remembered for two things. First they brought guns which the Japanese soon learned to make and use. And they also brought Christianity. At first the religion was quite popular. By 1581 there were about 150,000 Japanese Christians, including several *daimyo* in the western island of Kyushu.

Osaka castle

Life in the towns

From their open-fronted shops the shopkeepers watched the world go by. There would be quarrelling *samurai*, pilgrims on their way to a shrine and farmers with bales of rice. Passers-by would sit for a while on the edge of the raised shop-floor to talk and look at the goods inside. Serious customers left their shoes outside and stepped up into the shop to buy silk or *sake*, ricebowls or fans.

ISOLATION AND PEACE 1603-1853

The Tokugawa were the shoguns for the next 250 years. Tokugawa Ieyasu moved his capital to Edo (modern-day Tokyo) and made strict rules to keep the peace. He made his 250 *daimyo* spend half the year in Edo. When they returned home they had to leave their wives behind as hostages. This was done to guarantee their loyalty. Ieyasu also gave favours to his most faithful *daimyo*.

A later shogun became suspicious of the many Europeans who were now in Japan. He was afraid of their power, so he made them all leave and banned Christianity. For over 200 years Japan cut herself off from the rest of the world. A few Dutch, Chinese and Korean merchants were allowed at Nagasaki. Some Japanese scholars read Dutch books to keep in touch with new ideas. Then in 1853 four American ships arrived demanding supplies and trade agreements. Another big change was on the way for Japan.

The busy main road from Edo to Kyoto was called the Tokaido. Today this journey takes 3½ hours by Bullet Train. In the Edo period it could take up to 30 days. There were few bridges and many check-points. This made it impossible for *daimyo* armies to move in secret to attack the shogun.

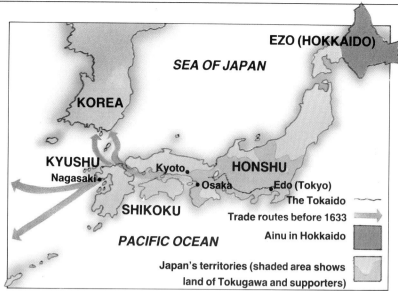

DATECHART

1603 Tokugawa Ieyasu becomes Shogun. He makes his headquarters at Edo. He also builds Nijo Castle in Kyoto to show his power to the Emperor.

c1603 *Kabuki* theatre develops. At first the plays are performed by women, but later men take over.

1609 The Dutch establish a trading post at Hirado.

1616 Ieyasu dies. He is buried in the famous Shinto shrine at Nikko.

1635-1639 Laws are made to stop Japanese from travelling abroad and foreigners from landing in Japan. Christianity is abolished.

1641 The Dutch traders are moved to Deshima Island near Nagasaki. Raw silk, sugar and medicines are imported.

c1635 The rise of big merchant families, such as Mitsui which now owns many banks and department stores.

1657 Edo is destroyed by fire.

1687 The Genroku Period begins. It is a time when town life flourishes and the *Kabuki* and *bunraku* puppet plays become more and more popular.

1694 The poet Basho dies.

c1720 The Japanese begin to import Dutch books.

1774 First translation of a Dutch book and growth of 'Dutch Learning'.

c1794-1840 Flourishing of famous wood-block artists.

1853 Arrival of American ships – the first "Black Ships". Their commander Commodore Perry demands trade with Japan.

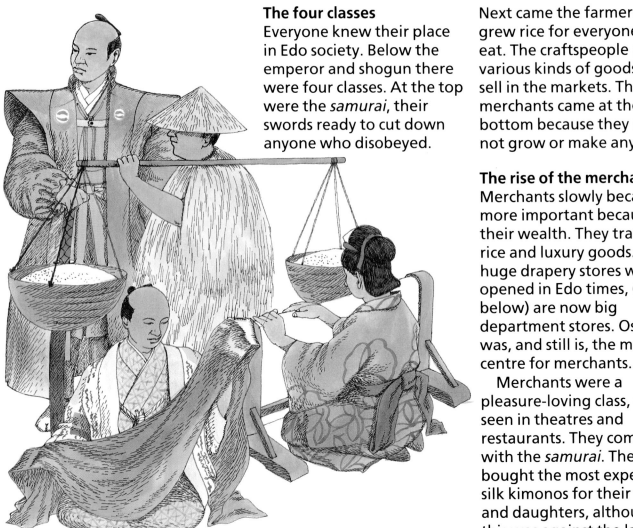

The four classes
Everyone knew their place in Edo society. Below the emperor and shogun there were four classes. At the top were the *samurai*, their swords ready to cut down anyone who disobeyed.

Next came the farmers who grew rice for everyone to eat. The craftspeople made various kinds of goods to sell in the markets. The merchants came at the bottom because they did not grow or make anything.

The rise of the merchants
Merchants slowly became more important because of their wealth. They traded in rice and luxury goods. The huge drapery stores which opened in Edo times, (see below) are now big department stores. Osaka was, and still is, the main centre for merchants.

Merchants were a pleasure-loving class, often seen in theatres and restaurants. They competed with the *samurai*. They bought the most expensive silk kimonos for their wives and daughters, although this was against the law.

Arts and craftspeople

Many beautiful articles made by Edo craftspeople still survive today. Apprentices learnt their crafts from masters who belonged to guilds. Each guild had a rich patron, for example, a rich priest who looked after it.

There were craftspeople who made swords, pottery, *tatami* floor-mats, fans and lacquerware – wooden articles with a hard, shiny surface made of resin.

Making cloth was a long and difficult process. The raw materials had to be spun, woven and dyed. Silk was worn only by the rich. Common people wore cotton dyed with patterns in indigo, a blue dye.

Buildings

All Japanese buildings used to be made of wood. Fire was a big danger. Houses had shutters to keep off the rain and snow. People changed from their outdoor shoes before stepping inside. Floors were covered with *tatami* mats made of rice straw for sitting and sleeping on. Houses, like the one in the photograph, were cold because of sliding doors and poor heating.

Today Japanese people still change their shoes when going indoors and modern houses keep many of the traditional features.

Poetry and cherry blossom

A poet called Basho developed *haiku* – poems with seventeen syllables about nature. Poets wrote about frogs, rain, the moon, mountains, the seasons and particularly cherry blossom.

Japan has rugged mountains, volcanoes and earthquakes. Life was sometimes hard and even dangerous. Life could also end unexpectedly. The beauty of the cherry blossom, which came and went so quickly, reminded people of the uncertainty of life. They went for picnics under the cherry trees to enjoy their brief beauty.

Education

There were a few schools in the 16th century. But during the peaceful Edo period, many more children went to school.

The *daimyo* set up new schools for the sons of *samurai*. The main subject for study was Chinese texts. Long hours were spend practising calligraphy (brush-writing). Chinese ideas of loyalty, martial arts and good manners were also taught. *Samurai* girls learned the arts of flower arrangement and the tea ceremony from their mothers. This would help them find good husbands.

Many commoners' children in villages and towns also went to school to learn reading and writing. Craftspeople's sons learned from their fathers or masters.

Entertainment

We can learn about leisure in the Edo period by looking at the many wood-block prints and paintings which still survive. They are called *ukiyoe*, or floating world pictures.

Some of these show scenes from the popular *kabuki* plays about revenge and love. The female parts were all played by men. Modern performances in Tokyo (photograph right) have not changed much since Edo times.

Other pictures show the ancient sport of *sumo* wrestling (right). There are also pictures of beautiful women from the pleasure quarters of Edo and Kyoto. This was the "floating world" where rich men went to forget their problems. They ate, drank and talked with the women called *geisha*.

OPEN TO THE WORLD 1853-1980s

The Americans and other foreign arrivals forced Japan to open her ports which had been closed for over 200 years. Japan felt weak compared with Western nations. The emperor was given back his power in order to modernise the country and build up its strength. Japan learnt from Western countries and introduced modern reforms. *Samurai* and the class system were abolished. An industrial revolution took place. Many people left their farms to work in factories.

As Japan modernised, it also strengthened its armed forces. Like Western countries it used them to build up an empire. But it lost this empire when it was defeated in World War II. Since the war Japan has made friends with former enemies and has worked hard on economic recovery and growth. Now it is a leading world power and one of the world's most technologically advanced nations.

In 1964 Japan hosted the Olympic Games in Tokyo. Over 90 nations took part and for the first time modern Japan was on show to the whole world. At the opening ceremony a Japanese athlete carried the Olympic Torch.

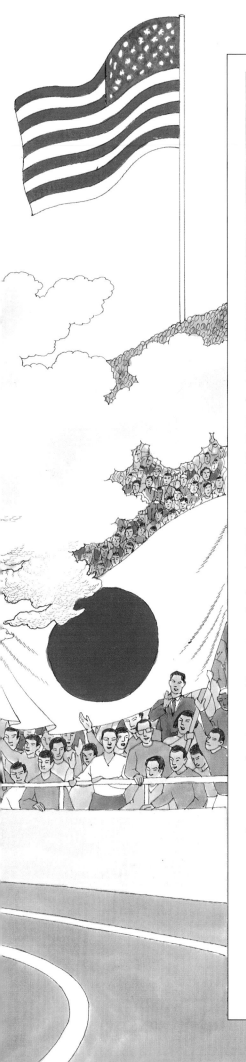

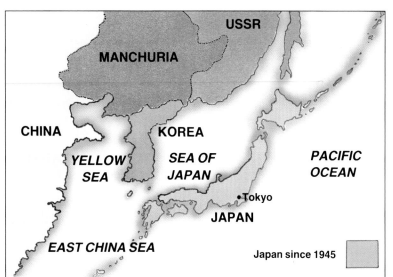

DATECHART

1854-1858 Japan makes treaties of Trade and Friendship with the United States, Britain, Russia, France and Holland.

1862-1868 A period of unrest with some violence between Japanese and foreigners. Armed Japanese rebellion against the treaties.

1868 Restoration of the Emperor Meiji. End of Shogun rule.

1870s Japanese study foreign ideas and advanced engineering. Education for all.

1889 The Emperor Meiji grants New Constitution.

1890 The first parliament meets. It is called the Diet.

1894-1895 War with China.

1904-1905 War with Russia.

1910 Japan colonises Korea.

1931-1945 Japan invades Manchuria and China and fights the United States and her allies in World War II.

1945 Japan surrenders after atomic bombs are dropped on Hiroshima and Nagasaki.

1945-1952 Occupation of Japan by Allied Forces.

1946 The New Constitution gives new laws and rights.

1946-1964 Economic recovery and rapid growth of incomes.

1956 Japan enters the United Nations.

1964 Tokyo Olympics

1979 Tokyo Economic Summit attended by leading world powers.

1985 Expo '85 in Tsukuba.

The Black Ships

In 1853 the sight of four strange American ships – the first "Black Ships" – was a big shock to the Japanese. Soon more ships arrived from other countries, such as Britain and Russia. These countries demanded the right to trade with Japan. The Shogun signed treaties with each of them giving them special favours. Foreign officials arrived to live and work in Japan. Strangely-dressed foreigners were often seen in Yokohama. The Japanese watched them carefully. Some even began to try out Western clothes.

Learning from the West

Emperor Meiji left Kyoto and travelled with great ceremony (illustrated right) to Edo which he renamed Tokyo, meaning eastern capital. He promised to make Japan a strong modern nation by learning from other countries.

Japanese people went to the United States and Europe to study. Foreign engineers and teachers were welcomed in Japan. Using Western models, the Japanese set up new systems of government and education. The photograph (right) shows an early meeting of parliament. Western clothes, food and arts also became popular.

any Japanese feared
ese foreigners. They
ticised the Shogun for
ving in to them. Finally
e Shogunate was abolished
d in 1868 the Emperor
gained his power.

War and peace

Japan won wars against China in 1895 and Russia (below) in 1905. It supported Britain and its allies in World War I.

In the late 1920s, army leaders took control of the government. They planned to extend Japan's empire all over east Asia and drive out the Westerners. Japanese armies invaded Manchuria in 1931 and China in 1937. In 1941 Japan entered World War II with an attack on the USA. Defeat finally came when the USA destroyed Hiroshima and Nagasaki with atomic bombs. Over 150,000 people were killed. Now thousands of people visit memorials like the Peace Dome in Hiroshima (bottom). Since the war Japan has armed forces for defence only and works for world peace.

The economy

By 1930 Japan was a fully industrialized country producing chemicals, machinery, silk and cotton. But during World War II all the factories were destroyed.

Japan recovered very quickly. In 1970, millions of people visited the world industrial exhibition, Expo '70 at Osaka, when Japan's progress was at its height.

Japan's main problem today is lack of raw materials, so it imports oil for energy and iron ore. It is a leading producer of cars, ships, iron, steel and TVs and trades all over the world. The old silk mills look very different from modern factories where robots do the dangerous work.

New technology

Japan is now moving away from heavy industry and into high-technology – products which rely on compact precision engineering. The Japanese are considered to be world leaders in "high-tech". Big developments have been made in robotics, advanced computers, energy, space research and medicine.

In Japan's space programme three astronauts, including a woman, are being trained for the first Japanese manned space flight. Japan often does research with other countries. For example, Britain and Japan produced the space satellite which was launched from Kagoshima in 1987 (right).

Family and home

Japanese houses today are quite small because building land is scarce. However, they have many labour-saving machines and nearly everyone has colour TV. Most homes are a mixture of Japanese and western styles. Japanese food is beautifully served in small bowls and eaten with chopsticks.

In Japanese families the wife is generally in charge of the children and their education while the husband goes out to work. However, things are changing slowly as more mothers go out to work.

Many workers are employed by big Japanese companies which are themselves like families. These companies take care of their workers. In return, the workers usually stay with that one company until they retire.

In the past old people were looked after by their eldest son and his wife. Now, because houses are so small, many old people live in a separate house nearby. But they still meet their families very often. Our picture shows a family outing on a very special occasion. The women and older children are wearing their kimonos.

In many ways modern Japan looks like any other thriving Western country. It has huge cities with skyscrapers and department stores. Most Japanese wear Western clothes. They like hamburgers and coca cola. They watch videos and play golf.

However, traditions are still very much alive in Japan. Craftspeople work with clay and bamboo, wood and paper. On special occasions women put on their traditional kimonos to visit shrines. Rice and fish are important foods. There are *samurai* dramas, *sumo* and *kabuki* on TV. Many people practise martial arts or calligraphy as hobbies. Japan belongs to both East and West.

Tokyo

Tokyo has over eight million inhabitants. During the week many more people travel in to work. Most of Tokyo was rebuilt after World War II. It has several skyscrapers. The main shopping street, called the *Ginza*, (shown right), is closed to traffic on Sundays. People in holiday mood stroll up and down window-shopping.

International finance

Japan plays an important part in trade and financial organisations worldwide. Its currency (money called *yen*) is accepted everywhere. Now, because of its economic success, many foreigners deal on Japan's stock markets.

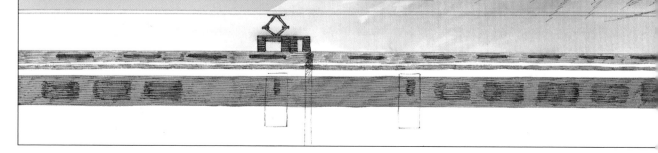

Enjoying the past

The top photograph (right) shows one of Japan's most famous festivals, the Gion Festival in Kyoto. It dates back to the 9th century. Crowds of visitors come every July to watch the splendid procession.

Japanese schoolchildren often visit famous places. These children (right) are visiting a Buddhist temple to learn about their country's history and culture.

The Shinkansen, or Bullet Train, is the world's second fastest train (210km/h).

INDEX

Photographic Credits:
Pages 9, 10, 26 and 27 (top):
International Society for Educational
Information; pages 16, 27 (bottom),
29, 30 and 31 (left and right):
Spectrum; page 20: Hutchison Library;
pages 23, 28 and 31 (bottom): Robert
Harding.